SECRETS

Published by: The Artists Archives of the Western Reserve
to accompany the exhibition of the same name

Designed by: Mindy Tousley
Contributors include:
Diane White-Tira and the estate of Marilyn Szalay
Judy Takács

Photography for Judy Takács is courtesy of the artist
Photographic portrait of Marlyn Szalay courtesy of William Pappas
All other photography is courtesy of the Archives

AAWR Support Staff:
Executive Director: Mindy Tousley
Gallery and Archives Coordinator: Megan Alves
Collections Registrar: Theodore Albano

AAWR Board of Directors:
Philip Bautista, President
Stuart Pearl, Vice President
David Joranko, Treasurer
Jocelyn Ruf, Secretary

Michael Bowen
Stephen Bucchieri
Lee Heinen
Stacy Swagger Hunter
Suzan Krause
Dr Vincent Monnier
Rota Sackerlotzky
John Sargent III

Copyright 2018 The Artists Archives of the Western Reserve
All Rights Reserved

SZALAY TAKÁCS SECRETS

May 24 - July 14, 2018

Presented by
The Artists Archives of the Western Reserve
1834 E 123rd St., Cleveland Ohio 44106

Front Cover image: Judy Takács detail from *Cancer Honeymoon* oil on linen triptych   30" x 46"
Back Cover image Marilyn Szalay detail from *Woodland Secrets II,* Conte crayon, chalk pastel on paper 32" x 40" 2004

AAWR would like to thank the following supporters:

The Bernice and David Davis Art Foundation
The George Gund Foundation
The William Bingham Foundation
The Zufall Foundation

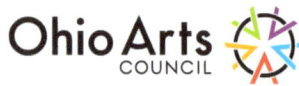

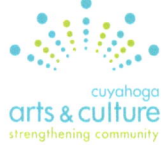

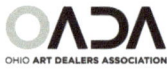

The Artists Archives of the Western Reserve (AAWR) is a unique archival facility and regional museum created to preserve representative bodies of work by Ohio visual artists.

Through ongoing research, exhibition, and educational programs the AAWR actively documents and promotes this cultural heritage for the benefit of the public.

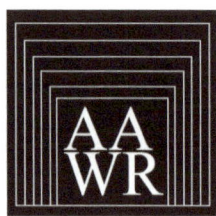

SZALAY TAKÁCS SECRETS

It is with great pleasure that the Artists Archives presents the inaugural exhibition, Secrets, for two newly Archived Artists, Judy Takács and the late Marilyn Szalay.

While these two artists differ, mainly in the choice of their respective mediums, their works share many similarities. They both choose to focus on the depiction of people as subject matter, at which they both excel. Each is concerned with capturing, not just a realistic portrait, but the psychological aspects of what lies beneath the surface. They each chose to photograph their subjects and make final drawings based on those photographs, and both have also used props on an ongoing basis when posing their models. The props then become symbols, metaphorical or allegorical, that add to the narrative of the finished work.

 Takács uses a variety of balls when posing her semi-nude models for her "Chicks with Balls" series, not only to help them hide their nakedness if they choose, but also as a metaphor for their strength and endurance. Judy's female subjects in this series have endured some form of physical, mental or emotional hardship and come out stronger on the other side. They are in her words, "The unsung heroines" of the Midwest. She repudiates the type of portraiture that smooths over the sitter's wrinkles and flaws and emphasizes instead the beauty of character earned by the hardship of life. These are the people you see every day on the street. Ordinary folk elevated by Takács' paintings into the status of mythical goddesses.

Marilyn Szalay used dolls, masks, shadow patterns, and reflections for maximum psychological effect in her drawings. She writes, "Like a stage director, I often create events which I photograph and then transpose into the larger drawings. I try to evoke a sense of the lives of the people who I photograph. Gesture and expression are essential to this portrayal of character." Szalay like Takács was in love with reality, and yet eager to show us evidence of the artist. It was important to her that, " My drawings are viewed as drawings with the vitality of hand drawn marks". Her sister Diane White-Tira, describes the incredible creative energy she brought to her life which is apparent in her work. Szalay's drawings of people capture frozen moments of time. There is a sense in some of her works that something has just happened or is about to happen, often leaving us with an impending feeling of unease or the foreshadowing of an unhappy event.

I would like to thank Judy Takács and Diane Tira for their help in organizing this show.
Judy did most of the heavy lifting on the curation of this exhibition. When I approached her to see if she was ready for her solo inaugural show as an Archived Artist it was her suggestion to include the works of Marilyn Szalay, who also was waiting for her inaugural exhibition. Judy also selected her own paintings without my help, designed a beautiful card for the show and contributed advertising, and writing for the Collective Arts Network publications. She even came up with the title, Secrets, which was a theme she found ran through both of their works. She and I together with Diane selected the work of Marilyn Szalay. While Judy probably didn't need me to help her with that aspect of the show, I confess I wanted the pleasure of looking through the works that Marilyn left behind when she passed away. That anticipated pleasure did not disappoint me. Diane patiently showed us sheet after sheet of exquisite drawings done by Marilyn and made our choices that much more difficult. While Marilyn drew animals extensively as well as people we chose to focus on the human portraiture, and included works drawn in a selection of different styles, for this exhibition pairing, while keeping in mind the theme of the title of the exhibition.

A special thank you to Diane White-Tira for recognizing and preserving her sister's artistic legacy by keeping this body of work intact. Celebrating and preserving the legacies of artists such as Judy Tacaks and Marilynn Szalay is why the Archives was formed and will continue.

Mindy Tousley
AAWR Executive Director

MARILYN SZALAY

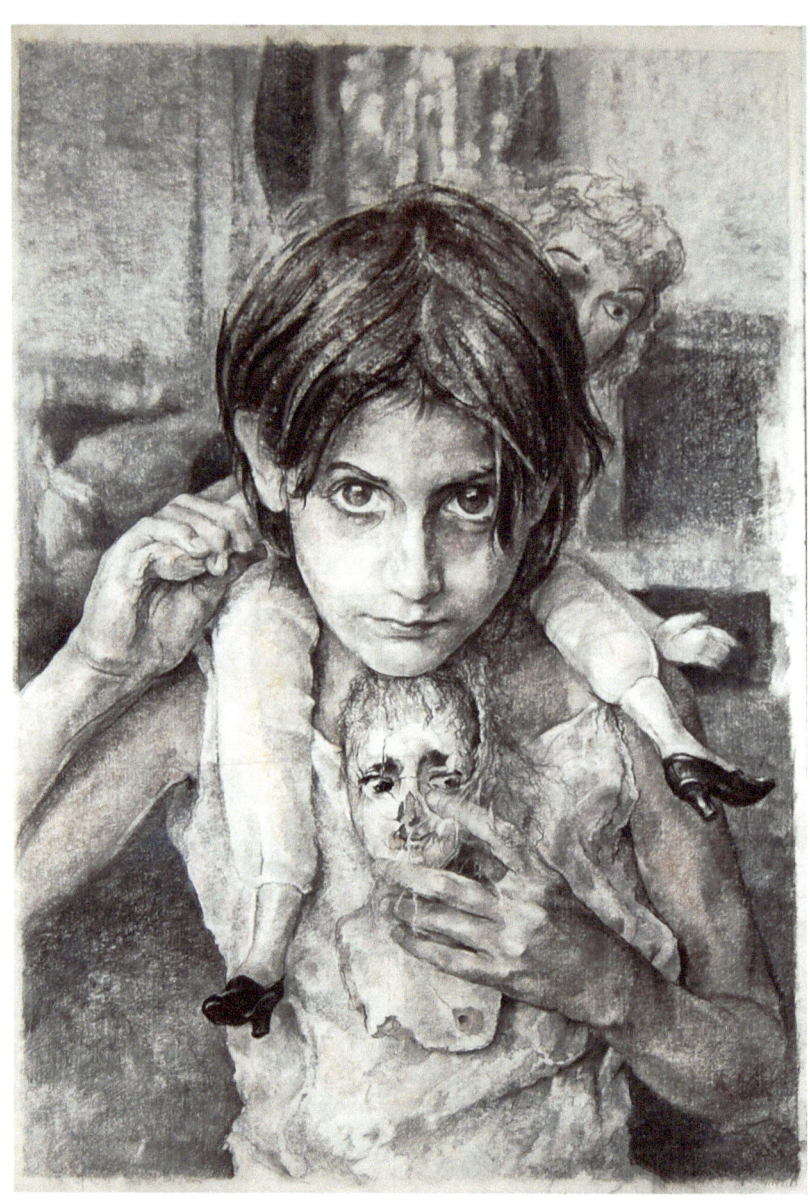

Mary Jane and Friends II   graphite, conte crayon, chalk pastel on paper   40" x 26"   1986
collection of Diane White-Tira

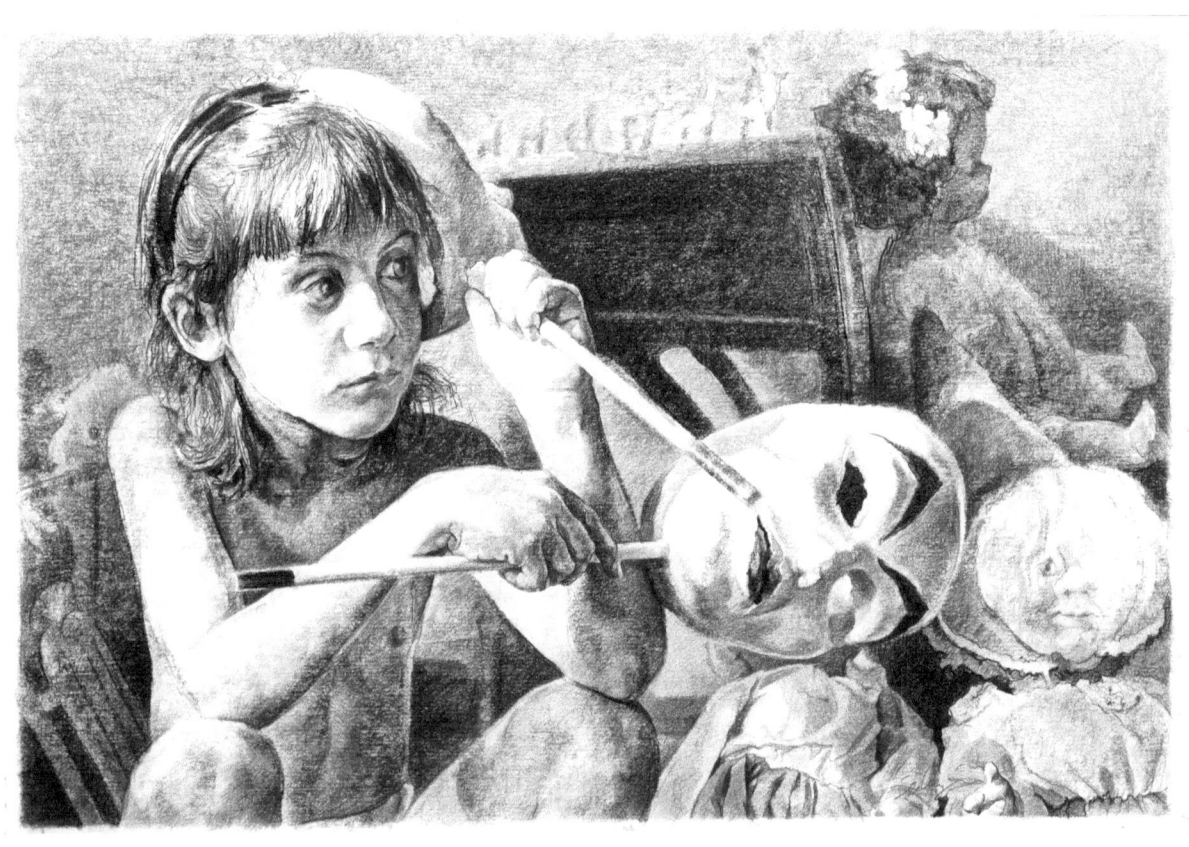

Childhood Dreams graphite, conte crayon, chalk pastel on paper 26" x 40" date unknown
collection of the Artists Archives of the Western Reserve

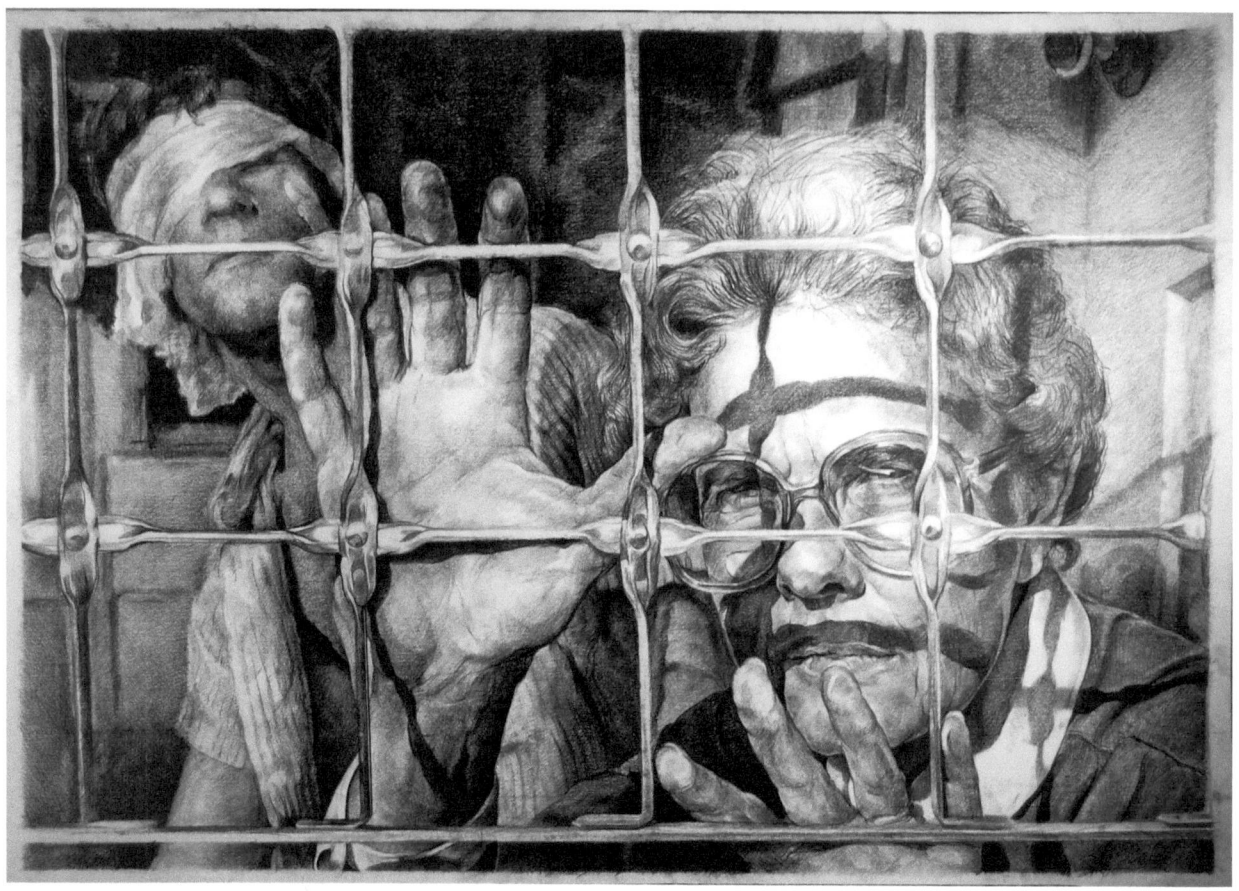

Mother, Son, Crisis   graphite, conte crayon, chalk pastel on paper   26" x 40"   date unknown
collection of Diane White-Tira

Artist Statement

I equate drawing with decision-making. For me, the process of drawing is complex. The more I draw and the more involved I am with the process, the greater the challenge becomes. Regardless of the type of imagery: literal or abstract, the same plastic concerns (issues of space, energy, light, etc.) must be resolved.

Drawing is a process of being alone. As I age and change, so does my awareness of drawing. My earlier marks were more frenetic, flying across the surface. Now they reflect contemplation. I am interested in the duality of organic vs. man-made shapes. When I create an image, it is the content to which I respond.

Trained as a painter, I changed paths after school to follow a career as a photojournalist. During this time, I discovered the exciting world that existed outside the studio. These instantaneous records of action, emotion and fleeting expressions and gestures were the energy of life that I sought to explore. However, I felt the flat grainy surface of a photographic print nullified the impact of these images.

Thus the transition from photography to drawing began. Drawing gives me the ability to contrast surface energy and to create intimate hand-drawn detail. The camera gives me free rein to portray the vitality of my subjects, as opposed to the often mundane images of the model posing in the studio.

And, the psychological ramifications of cropping and placing the human form within the confines of the rectangle, is a means of manipulating space for emotive purpose.

I continually redefine myself and my perceptual skills and view of humanity, whenever I draw. It is my fascination with the nature of things that binds me to actual imagery. The gaze of an eye or the gesture of a hand, in its myriad of variations, can be so powerful and captivating. By developing my acute sense of perception, I am open to the subtle yet infinite possibilities. My images are an intense and personal record of eternal moments in time.

This Statement was assembled from words Marilyn had written throughout the course of her career. Edited by her sister Diane White-Tira and Judy Takacs for "Majority Rising"

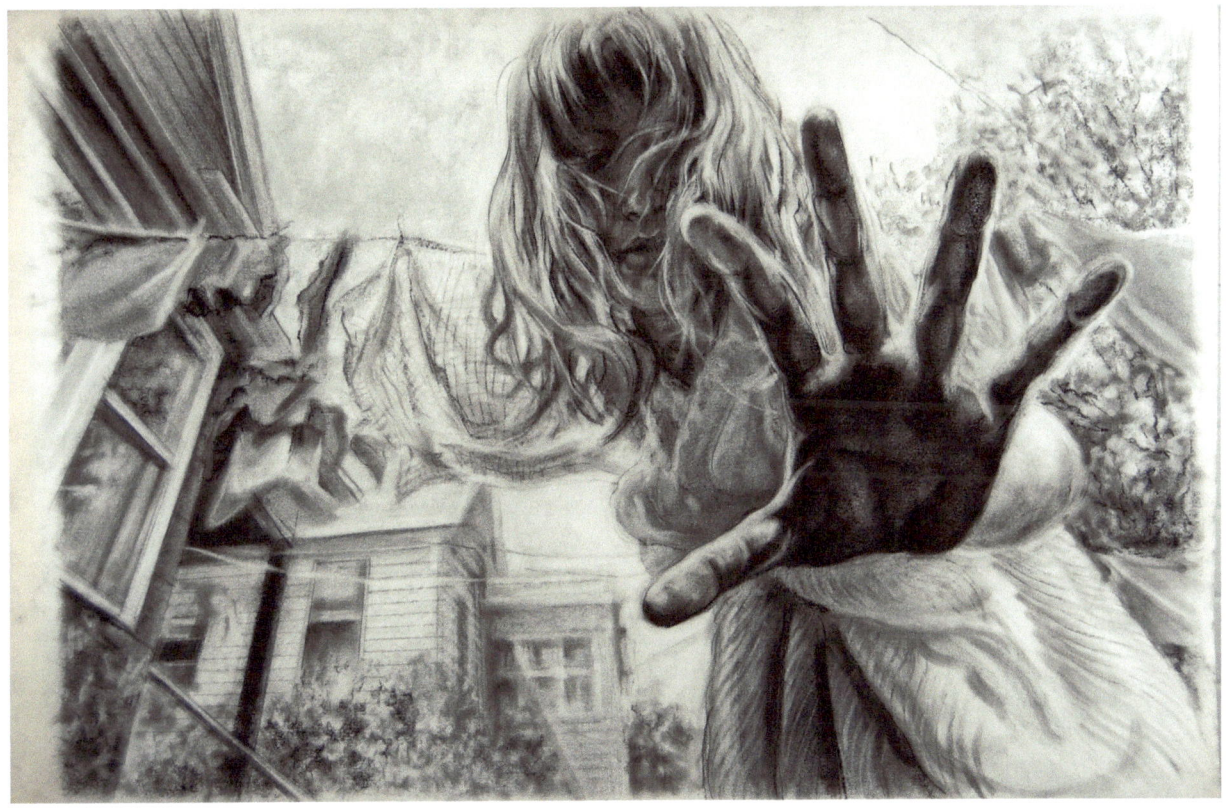

Untitled graphite, conte crayon, chalk pastel on paper   26" x 40"   date unknown
collection of Diane White-Tira

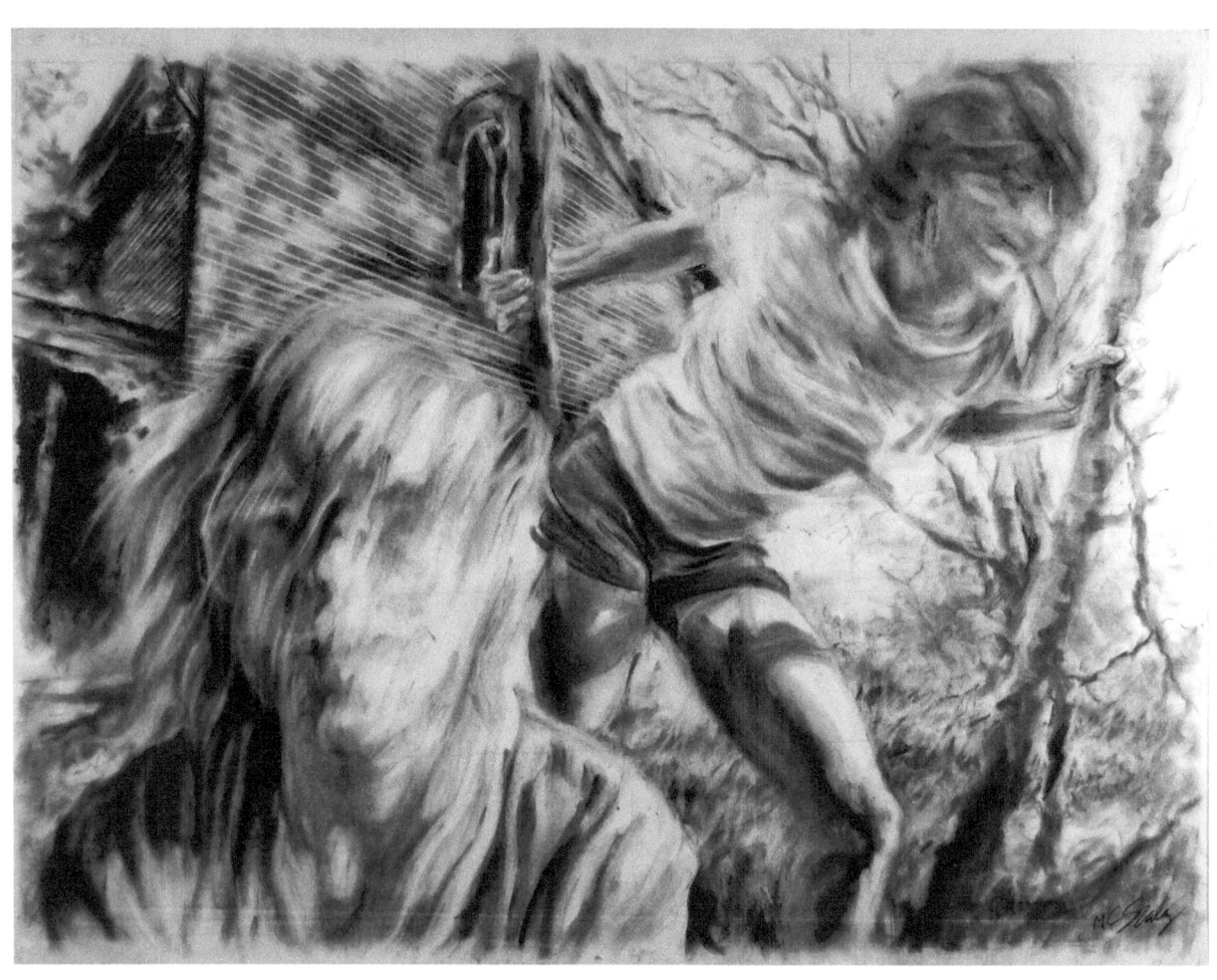

Untitled   graphite, conte crayon, chalk pastel on paper   32" x 40"   date unknown
collection of Diane White-Tira

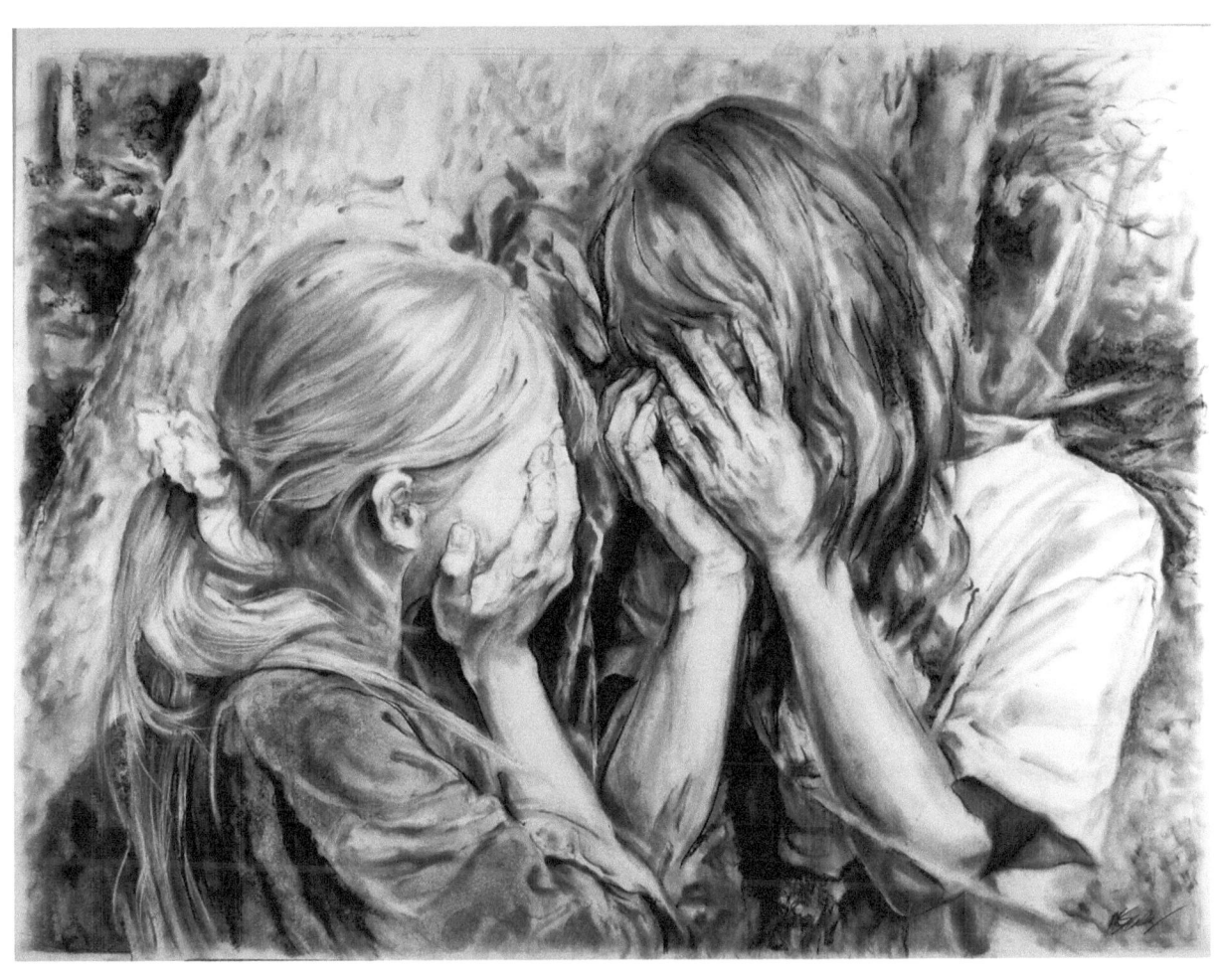

Woodland Secrets II   graphite, conte crayon, chalk pastel on paper   32" x 40"   2004
collection of Diane White-Tira

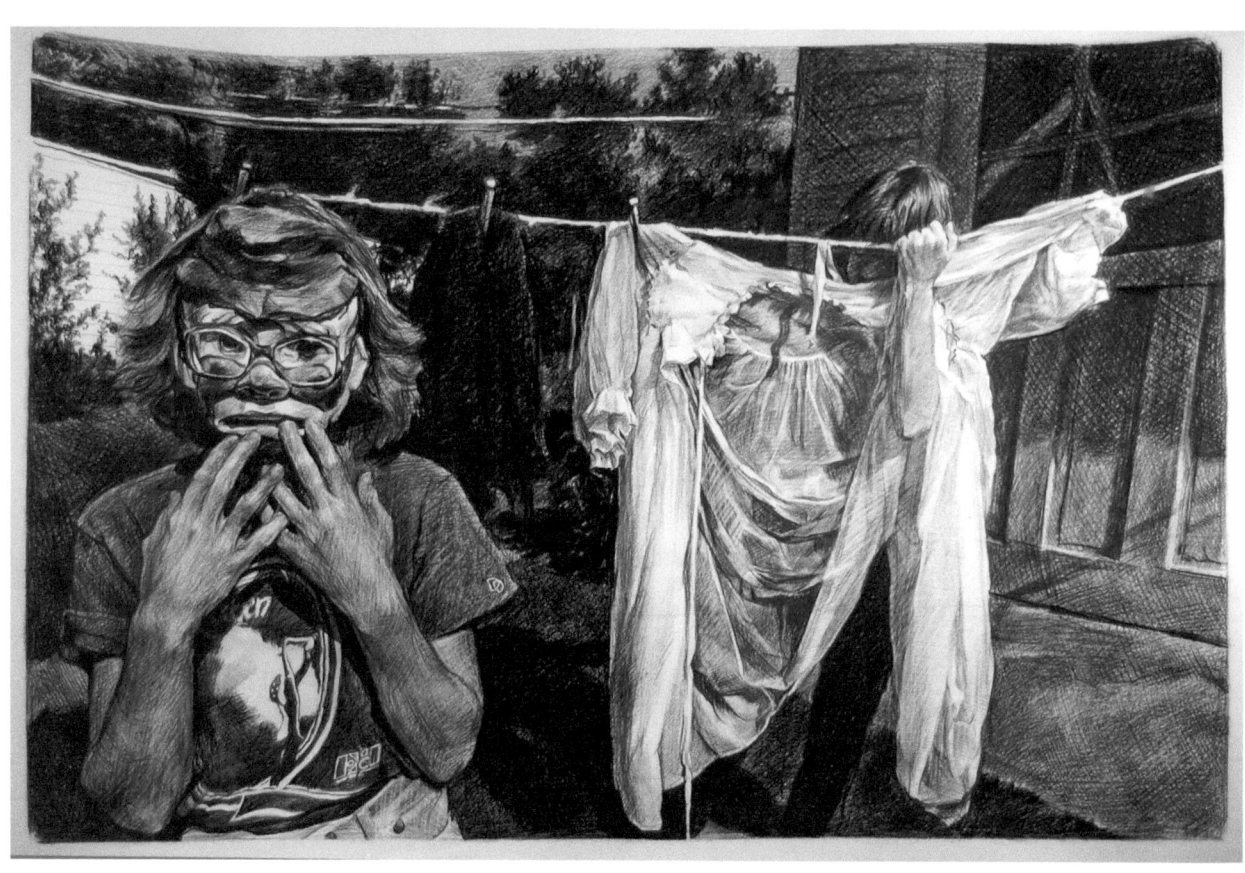

Untitled   graphite, conte crayon, chalk pastel on paper   26" x 40"   date unknown
 collection of Diane White-Tira

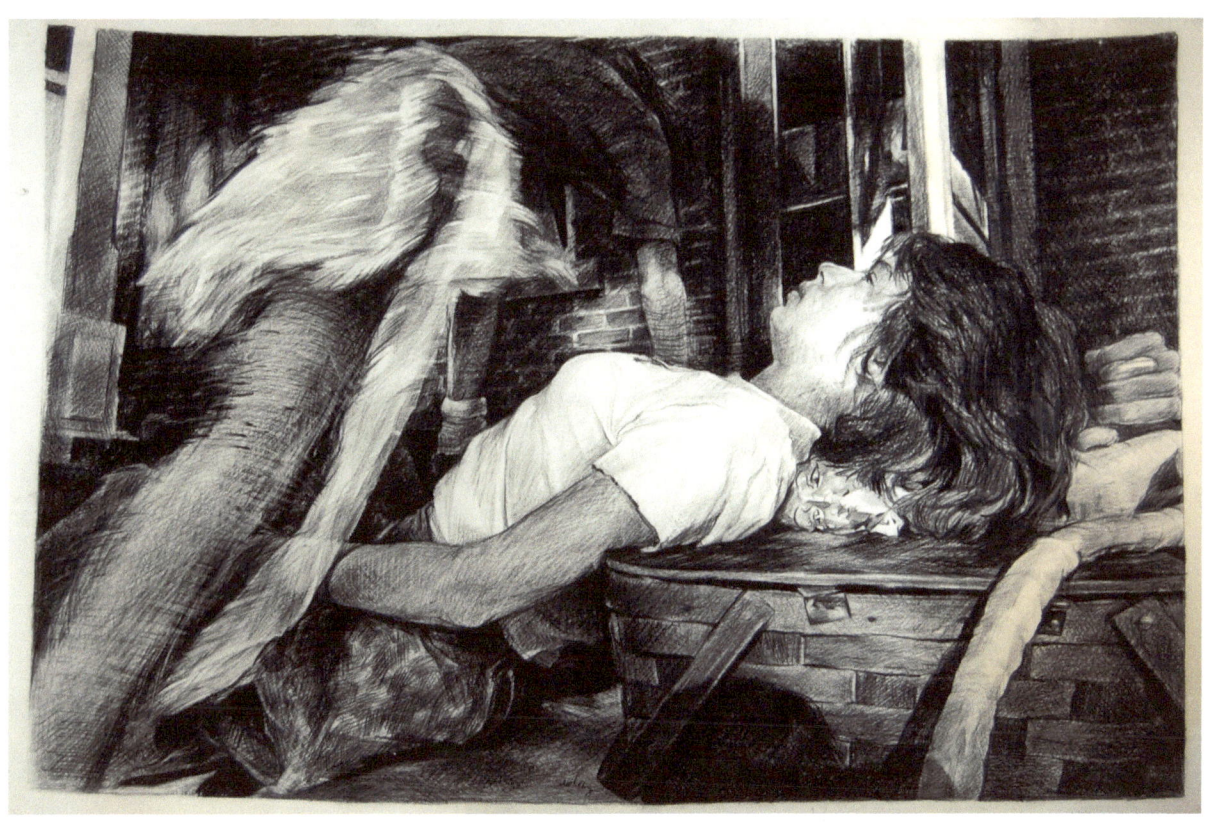

Homage to David II   graphite, conte crayon, chalk pastel on paper   26" x 40"   date unknown
collection of Diane White-Tira

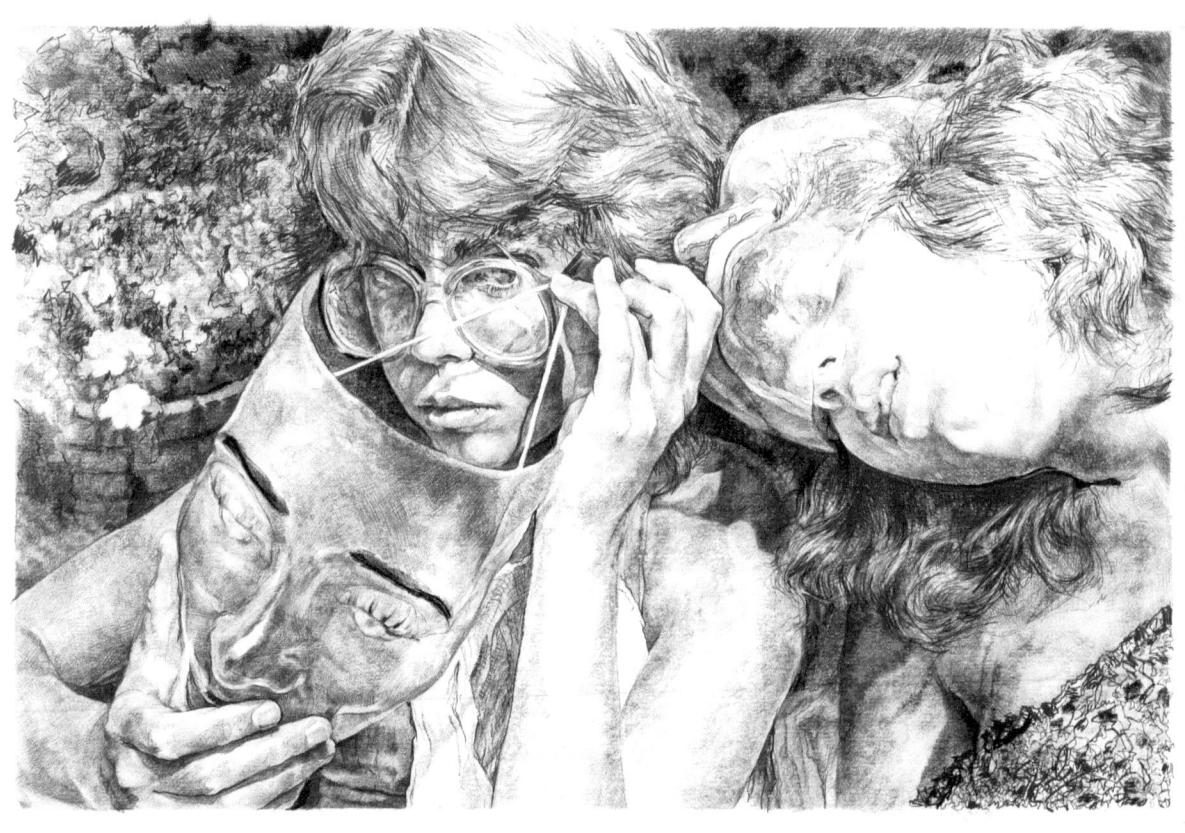

Tangible and Intangible   graphite on paper   26" x 40"   date unknown
collection of the Artists Archives of the Western Reserve

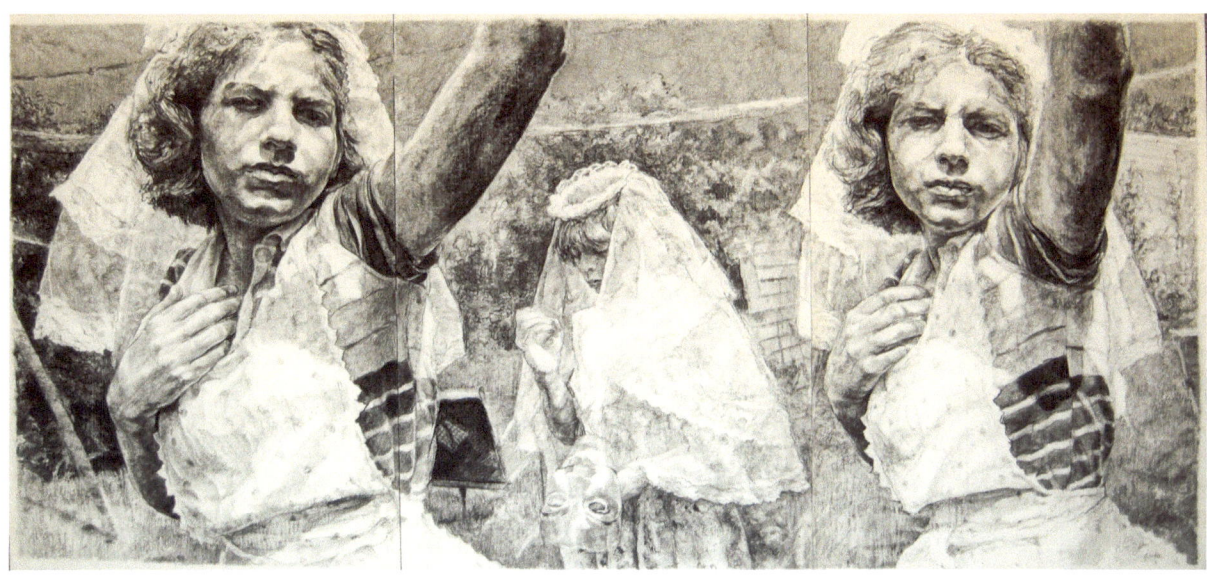

Rite of Passage graphite, conte crayon, chalk pastel on paper   40" x 78" (triptych, each panel 40" x 26")
date unknown   collection of Diane White-Tira

"My images are about girl changing to woman. I work primarily with adolescents because they reflect this transition and turbulence. I often use the disjointed juxtaposition of imagery to physically interpret this emotional conflict. Dual imagery also recalls the element of time which is rudimentary to this concept. A girl's dreams are a synthesis of universal intuition coupled with society's codes and models. Often, in becoming a woman, she either loses these dreams or becomes a victim of these social codes. Can the dreams meet with reality? My images are a continual exploration of this question."

M. Szalay

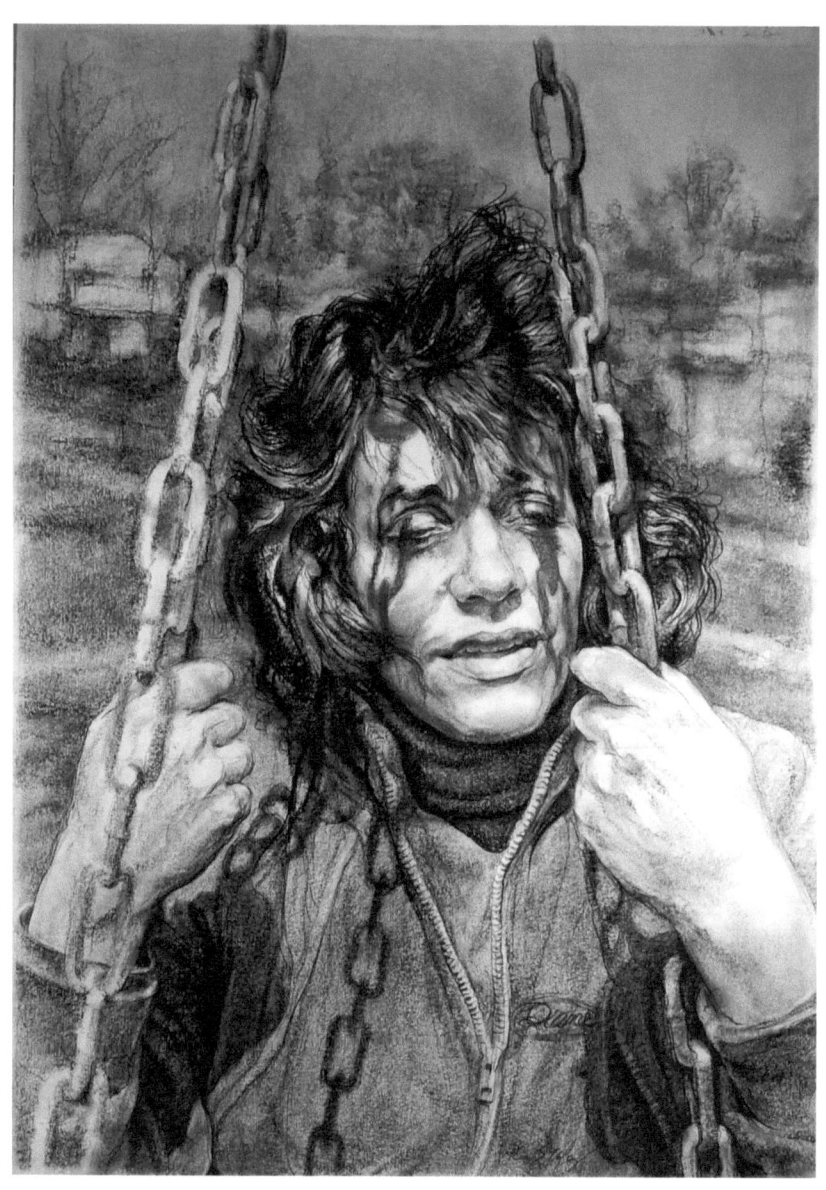

In Early Spring (portrait of Diane)   graphite, conte crayon, chalk pastel on paper   40" x 26"
date unknown   collection of Diane White-Tira

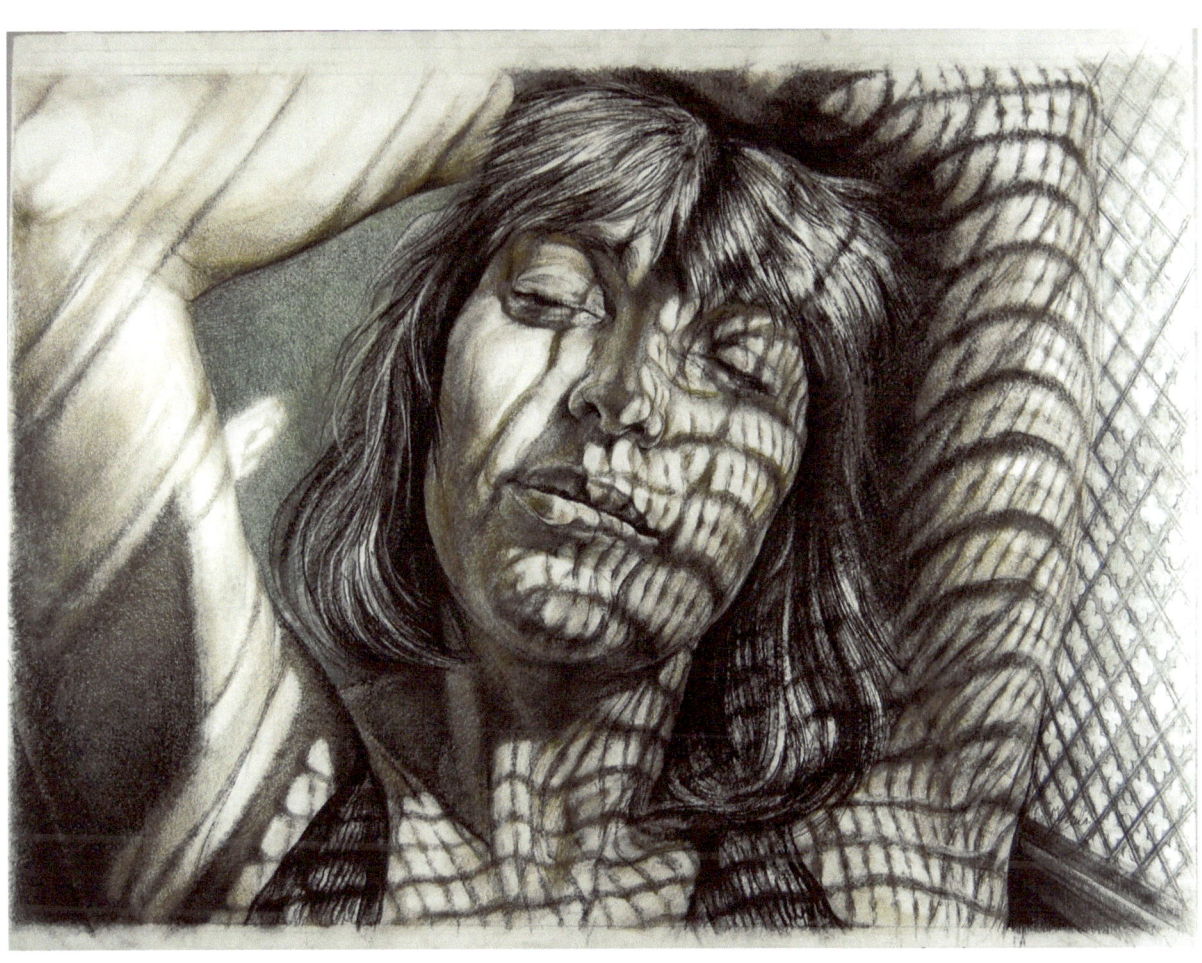

Untitled   graphite, chalk pastel, conte crayon on paper   32" x 40"   date unknown
collection of Diane White-Tira

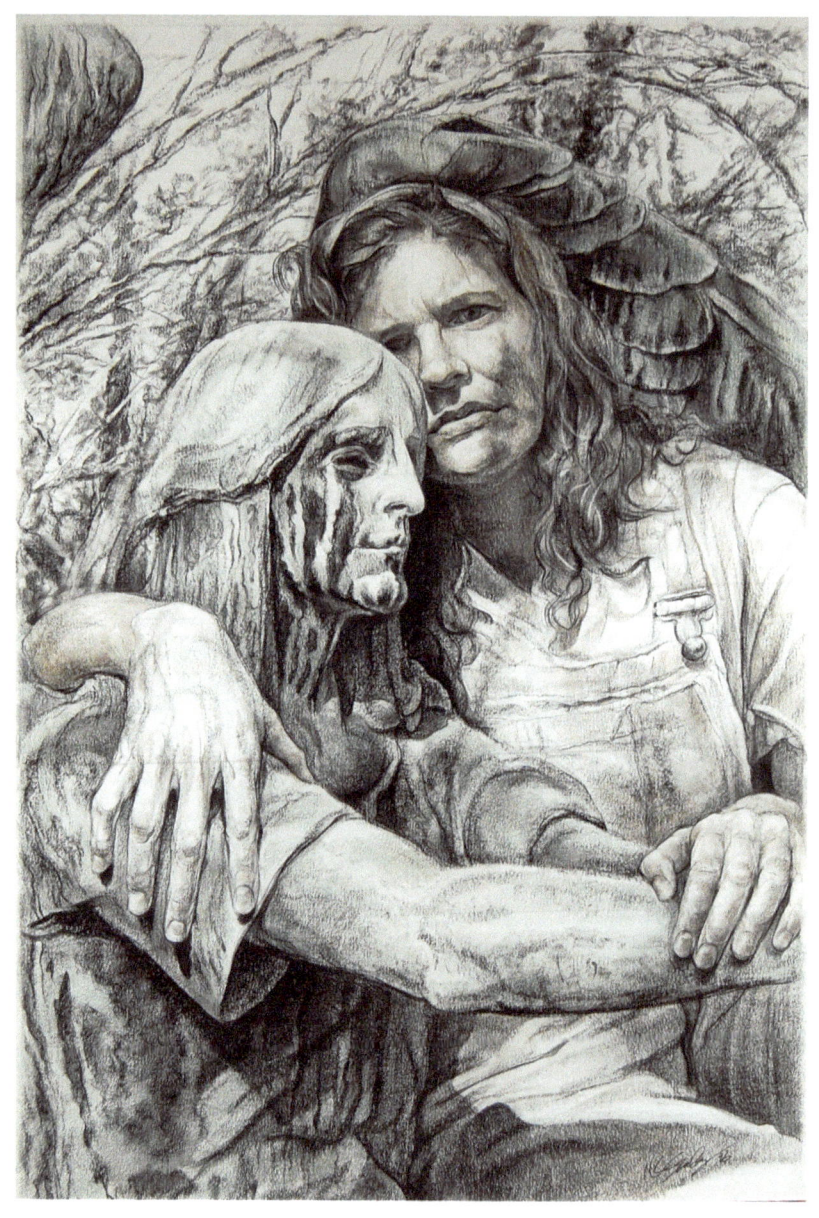

Guardian Angel   graphite, conte crayon, pastel on paper   40" x 26"   1996   collection of Diane White-Tira

JUDY TAKÁCS

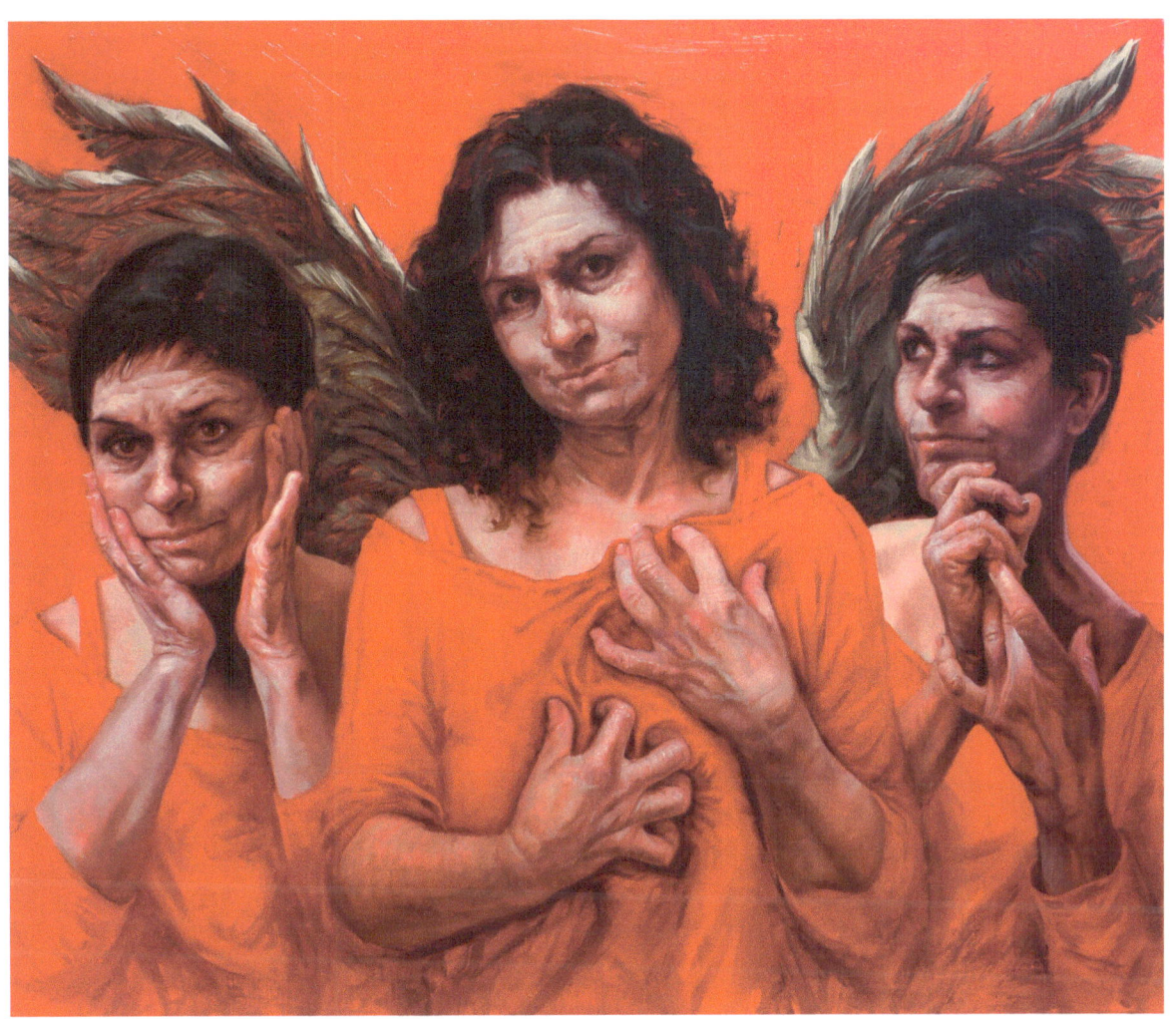

Guardian Angel of the Good Death   oil on linen   30" x 40"   collection of the artist

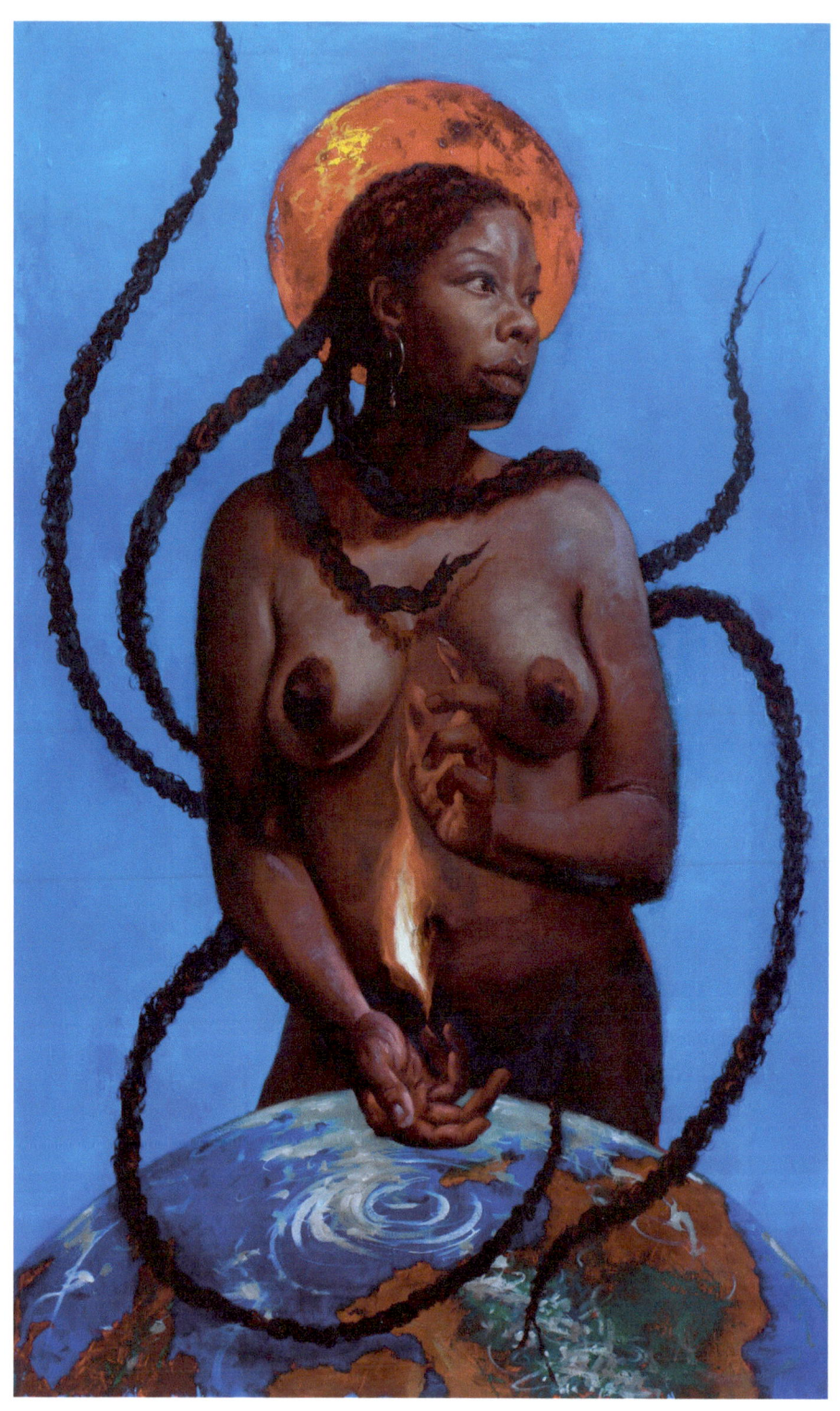

Venus, She's Got It oil on linen   48" x 30" collection of the artist

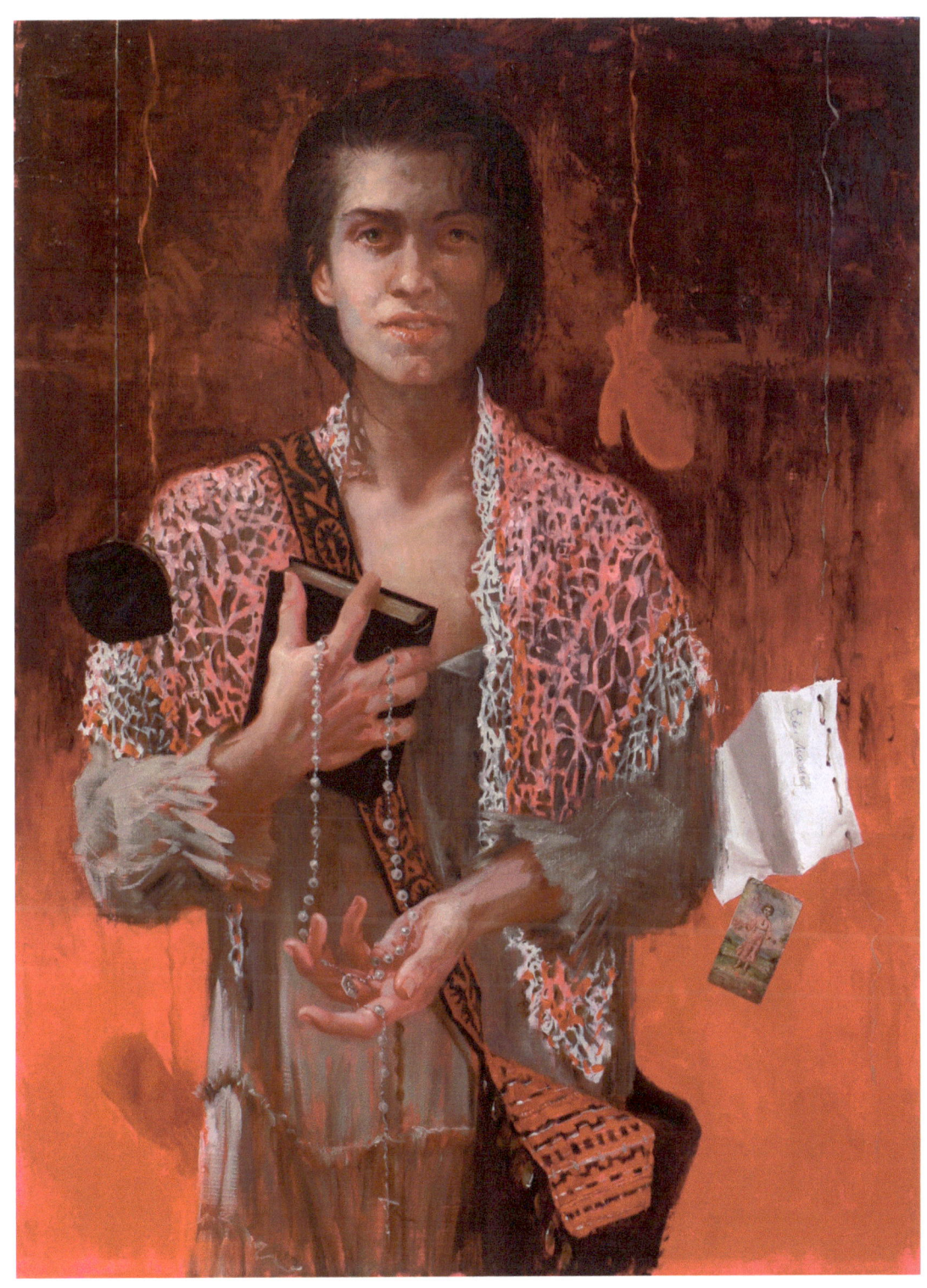

Titkos Testvér (Secret Sister) oil on linen 40" x 30" collection of the artist

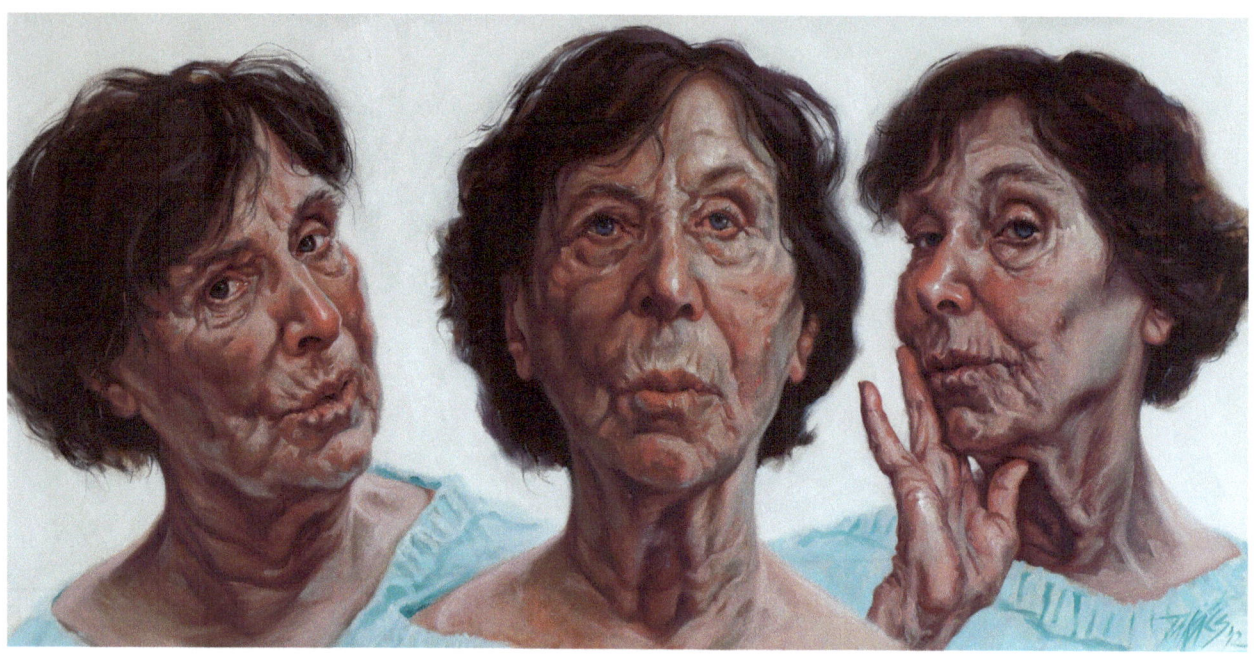

Judge, Jury and Executioner   oil on canvas   24" x 48"   collection of the artist

Artists Statement

My goal as an artist is to paint people in all their glory, with all their baggage, with their pride, with their pain, with their strengths, with their frailties, with sensitivity and with understanding.

Sometimes it is a family member who puzzles me, sometimes it is a posed model who symbolizes concepts I wrestle with, or happen upon as I paint. It is always people that find their way into my paintings…and it is their souls that hopefully find their way out.

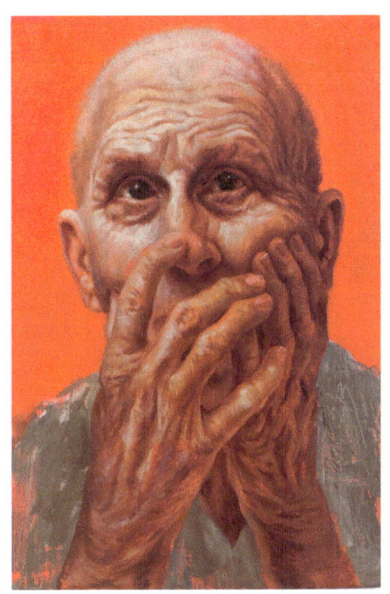 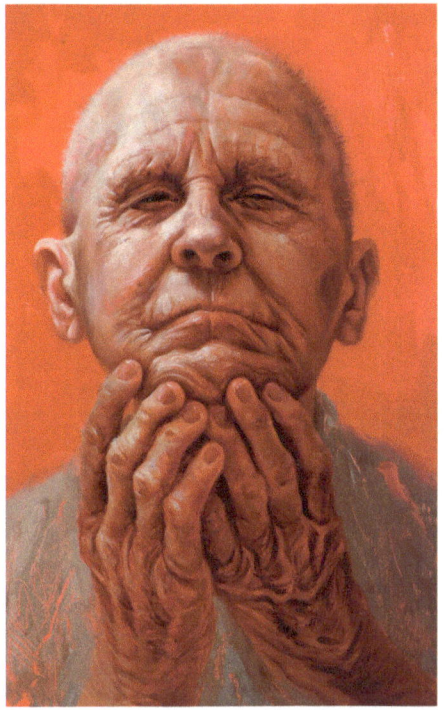 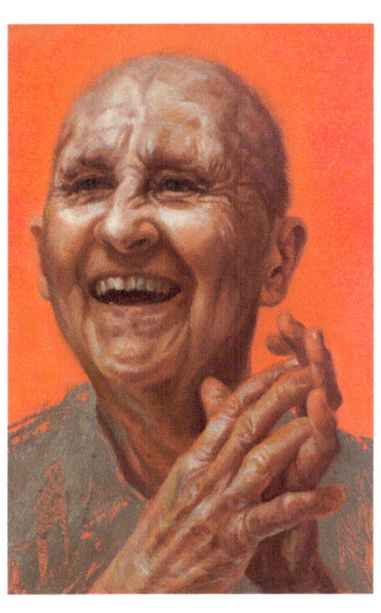

Cancer Honeymoon   oil on linen, triptych   30" x 46"   collection of the artist

Chicks with Balls Statement

Over the past few years I have been asking my female friends and family to take off their tops for me and pose holding a variety of balls to cover their breasts. Oddly enough, many of them said yes. Here's why, **these** chicks really do have balls, and not just the kind it takes to have a little fun and show some skin. They are truly the unsung heroines of their ordinary Midwestern lives…and the balls are literal as well as metaphorical. "Chicks with Balls" is the collection of paintings that resulted from these encounters.

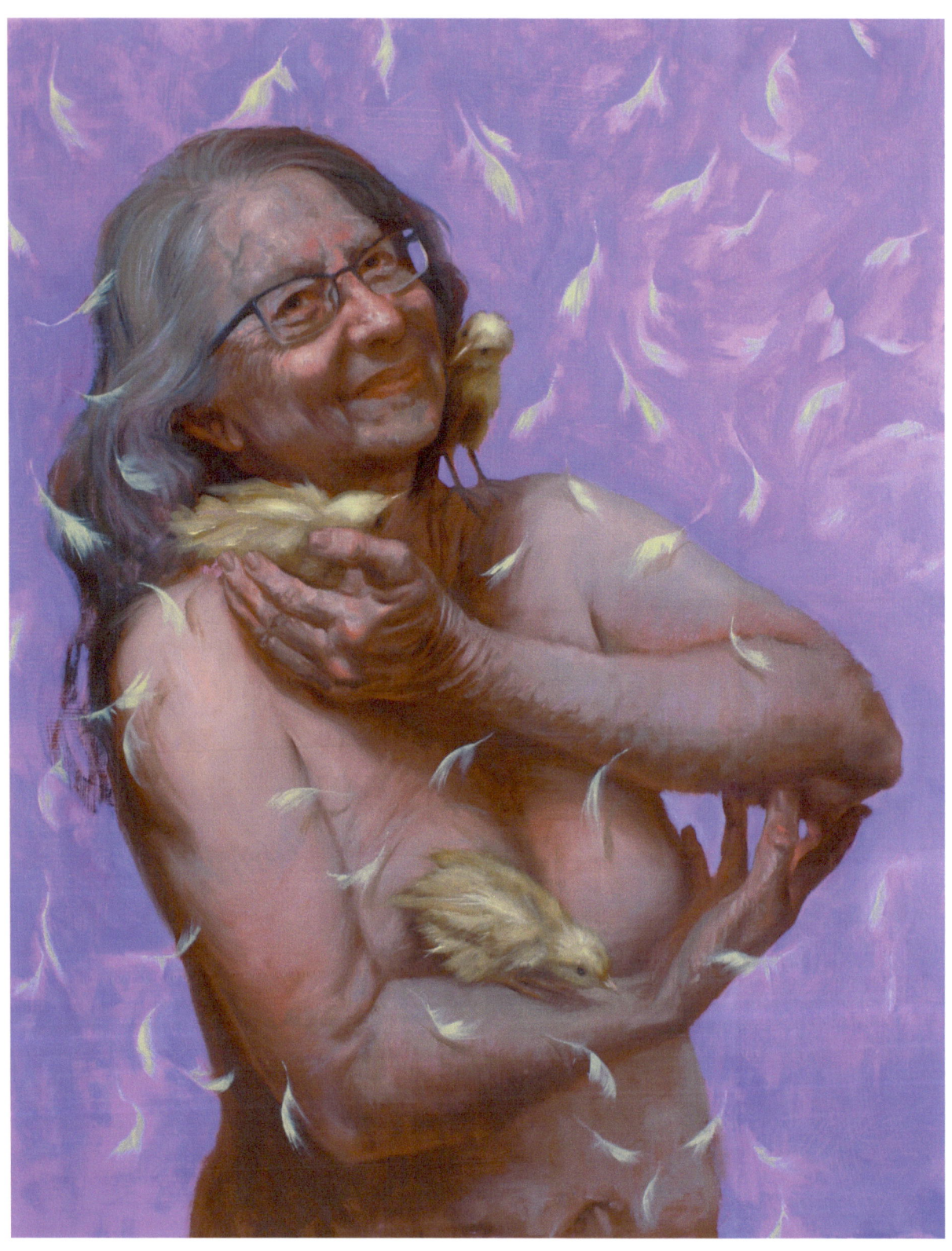

Carol Raises Chicks and Spirits   oil on linen   30" x 24"   collection of the artist

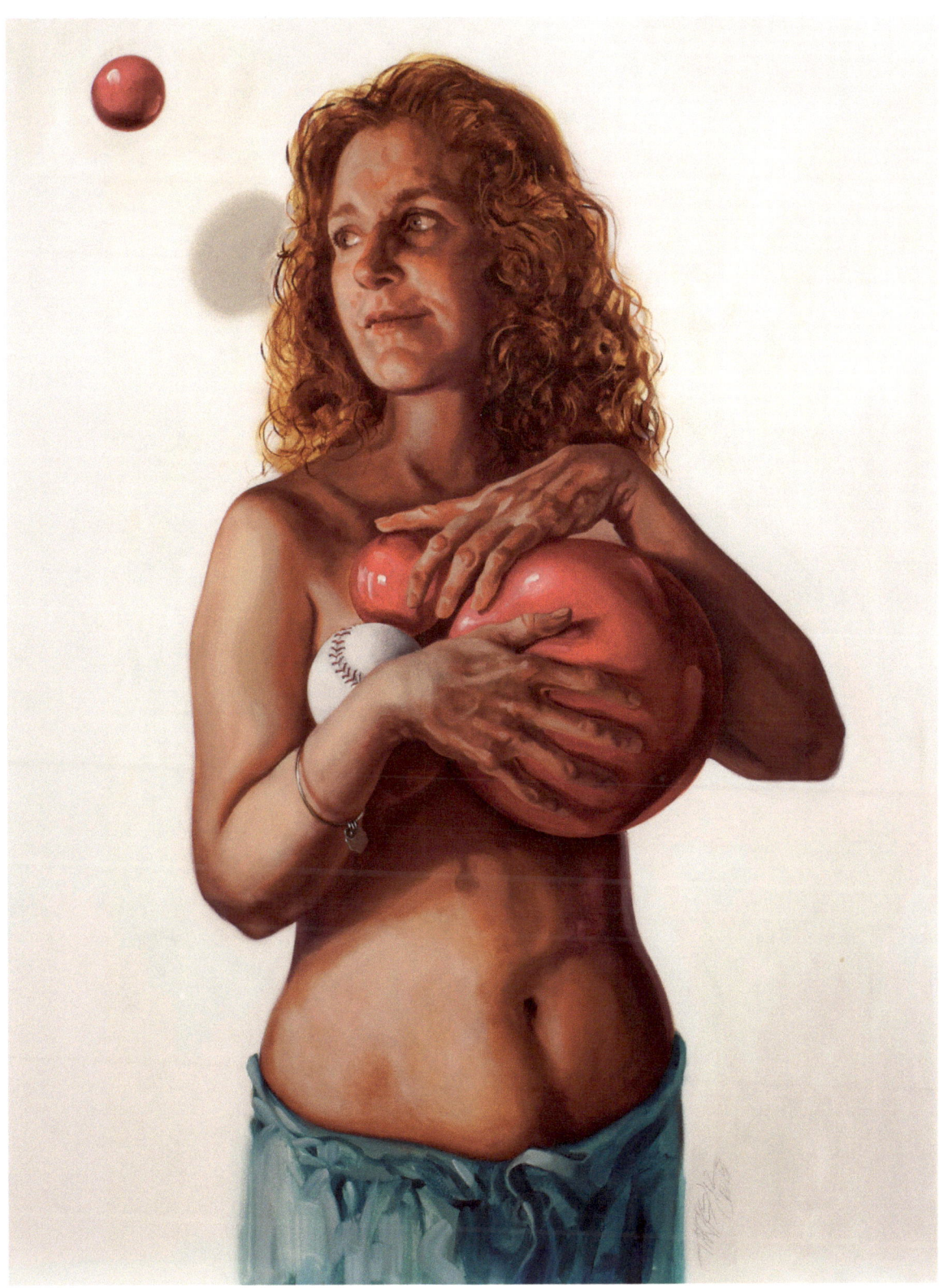

Nina is Grace under Fire oil on canvas 48" x 36" collection of the artist

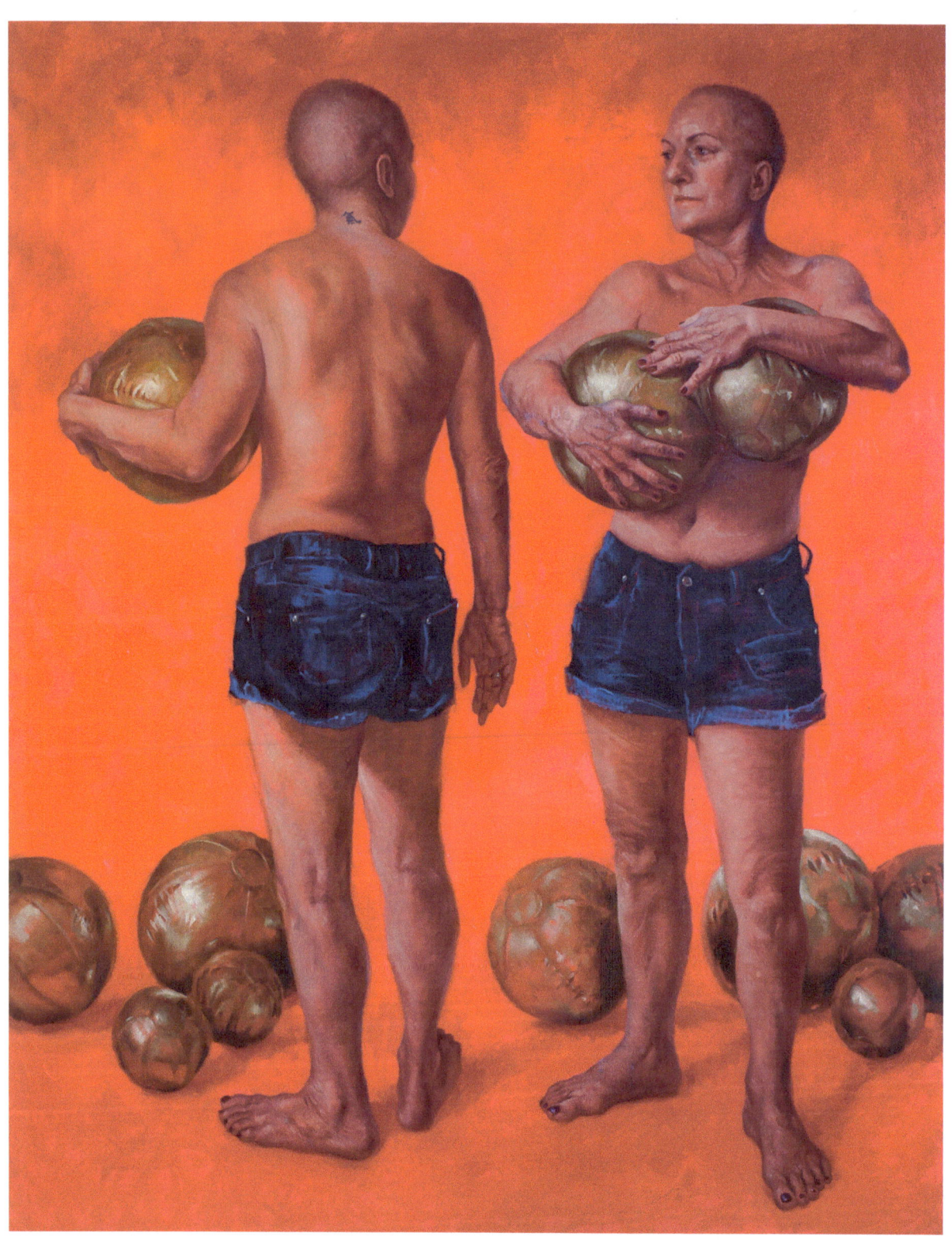

Blazine, Heart of Gold   oil on canvas   48" x 60"   collection of the artist

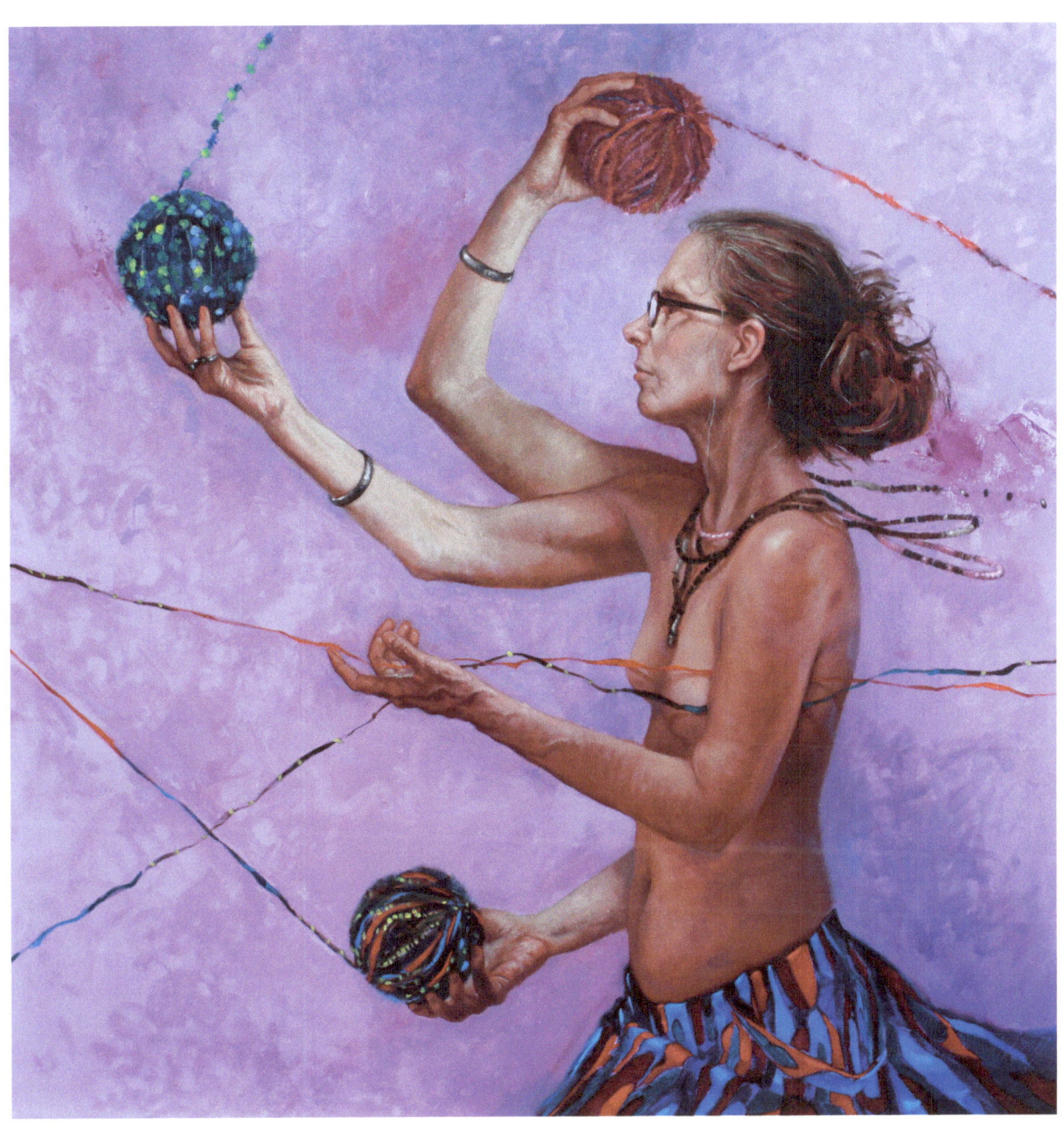

Kim, the Keeper of Time   oil on canvas   48" x 48"   collection of the artist

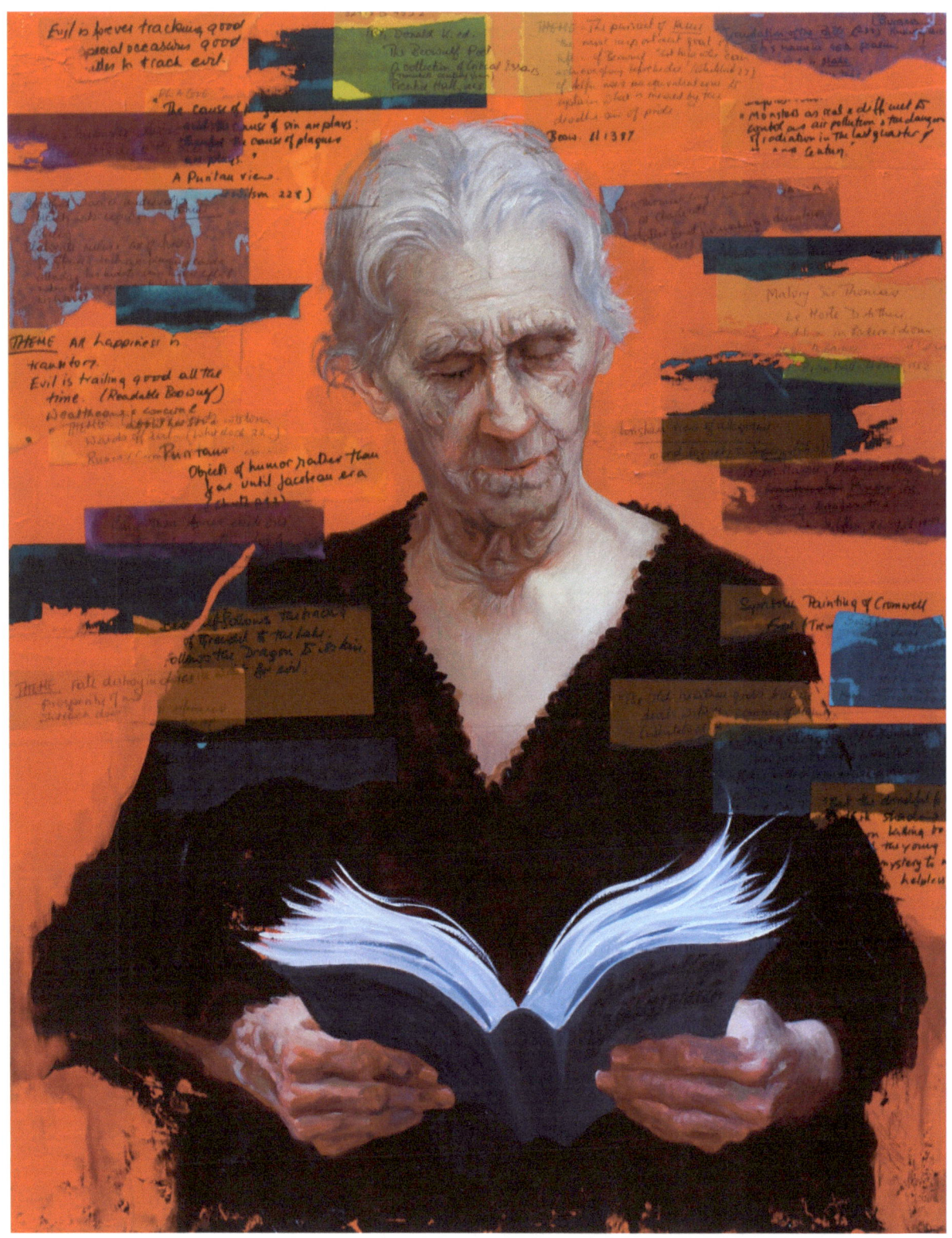

The Final Chapter (Két Világ Határán...Between Two Worlds) oil on linen 30" x 24" collection of the artist

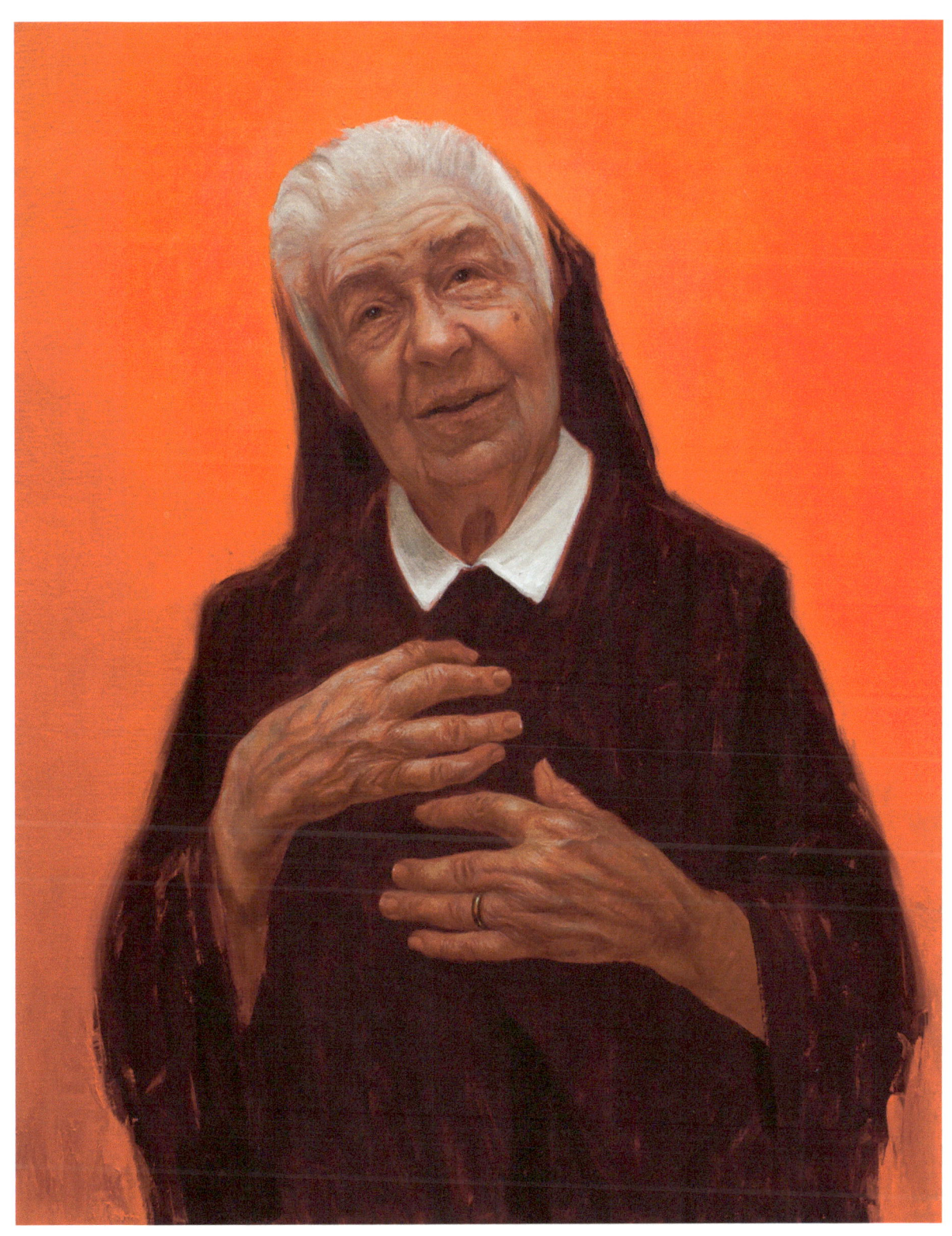

Conversation   oil on linen   30" x 24"   collection of the artist

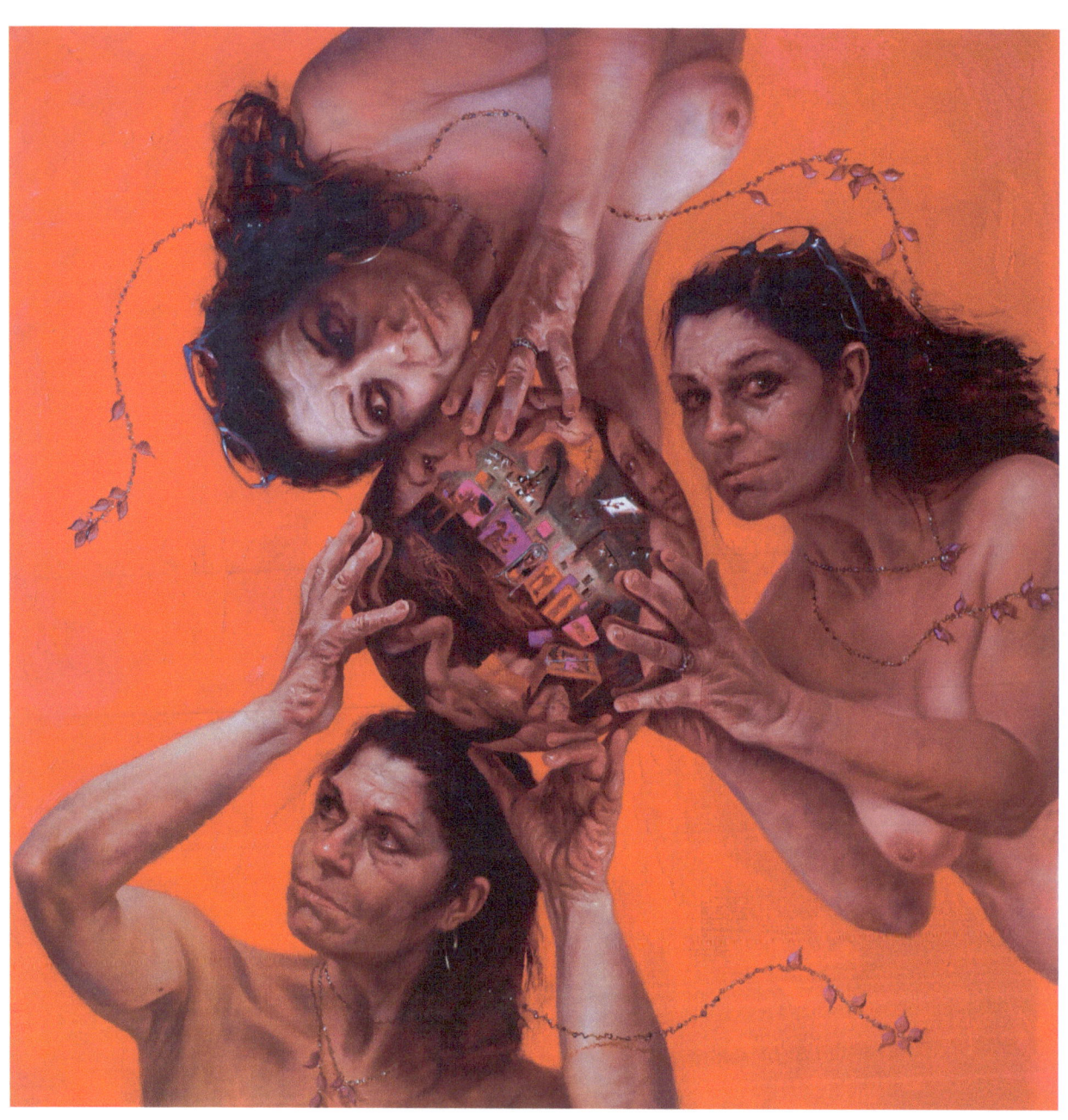

Judy, Judy, Judy oil on linen   40" x 40"   collection of the artist

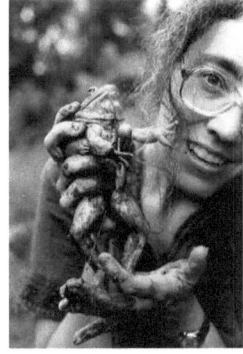

MARILYN SZALAY CHRONOLOGY
1950 - 2012

Education/Training

1972	Kent State University, Kent, OH, B.F.A.
1975	Kent State University, Kent, OH, M.F.A.

Professional Experience

1975	Kent State University, Kent, OH, Graduate Assistantship
1975-2012	Cuyahoga Community College, Cleveland, OH, Tenured Professor of Drawing, Painting, Design, Photography, Computer Graphics
1976-83	Sun News, Cleveland, OH, Photographer
1978	Cooper School of Art, Cleveland, OH, Instructor, Art
1979	Cleveland State University, Cleveland, OH, Instructor, Art
1979-86	Cleveland Ballet, Cleveland, OH, Photographer
1981-88	Southwest General Hospital, Middleburg Heights, OH, Photographer
1987-89 also 1994-1996	University of Akron, Akron, OH, Instructor, Art
1991-2004	Cleveland Institute of Art, Cleveland, OH, Instructor, Art
1992, 93	Cleveland Institute of Art, Cleveland, OH, *Project Pathways,* Instructor, Art
1993-96	Cleveland Metroparks Zoo, Cleveland, OH, Illustrator
1994	Akron Children's Hospital, Akron, OH, Animal Drawing Workshop, Teacher
	Cleveland Institute of Art, Cleveland, OH, Animal Drawing Workshop teacher
1994-2001	Orange Art Center, Pepper Pike, OH, Art Teacher
	Cleveland School of Art, Cleveland, OH, Artist in Residence
1994, 96	Virginia Marti College of Fashion and Art, Lakewood, OH, Instructor
1998-99	Kent State University, Kent, OH, Instructor, Art

Selected Exhibitions and Awards

1980	*Aitken, Keech and Szalay,* three-person show, SPACES, Cleveland, OH
1983	Faculty Exhibition, group show, University of Akron, Akron, OH
1984	*Drawings,* (an Exhibition of Fifteen Ohio Artists) traveling exhibition, SPACES, Cleveland, OH; Contemporary Art Center, Cincinnati, OH; Southern Ohio Museum and Cultural Center, Portsmouth, OH
	Spaces, Public and Private, group show, Valley Art Center, Chagrin Falls, OH
1985, 86, 90	May Show, Cleveland Museum of Art, Cleveland, OH; 1985 Cash Award, Graphics
1986	*Drawing on Time,* three-person show, Cleveland State University, Cleveland, OH
	All Ohio, group show, The Canton Art Institute, Canton, OH
	La Femme, group show, Gloria Plevin Gallery, Chautauqua, NY
1987	*Mauersberger and Szalay,* duo show, Cuyahoga Community College, Cleveland, OH
	A New Generation of Ohio Artists, juried show, Kent State University, Kent, OH, Purchase Award
1988	National Drawing and Painting Exhibition, juried show, The Hoyt Institute, New Castle, PA
1989	*Rogers, Gillette and Szalay,* three-person show, Butler Institute of American Art, Youngstown, OH

MARILYN SZALAY CHRONOLOGY CONT.

1990	*Ohio Artists: The Human Figure,* Canton Art Institute, Canton, OH
	Jewish Community Center, Purchase Award
1991	*Zoo Images,* Photographs and Drawings by M. Szalay, solo show, Trumbull Art Guild, Warren, OH
	Marilyn Szalay, Figurative Work, solo show, Mount Union College, Alliance, OH
1992	*Gorilla Giver Brochure,* Award of Excellence, Simpson Paper Co., Cleveland, OH
	27th Annual Photography Show, Jewish Community Center, Cleveland, OH; Artistic Excellence Award, Framart Merchandise Certificate
1993	*Women's Voices,* group show, Case Western Reserve University, Cleveland, OH
1996	*Drawing in Ohio at the Turn of the Century,* juried show, University of Akron, Akron, OH
	Annual Juried Show, Erie Art Museum, Erie, PA
1997	*The Allegorical Figure,* group show, Case Western Reserve University, Cleveland, OH
	Marilyn Szalay Drawings, solo show, Lakeland Community College, Kirtland, OH
1998	75th Annual Spring Show, Erie Art Museum, Erie PA
	A Fine Line, group show, Cleveland Artists Foundation, Cleveland, OH
1999, 2001	and 2003 *National Midyear Exhibit,* Butler Institute of American Art, Youngstown, OH; 2001 Juror's Mention Award
2000	*Realism Today,* national juried competition by *American Artist* magazine, John Pence Gallery, San Francisco, CA
2000, 2002	*The Russell Art Show,* Fairmount Fine Arts Center, Russell Township, OH; 2000 First Place Graphics; 2002 Honorable Mention Graphics
2001	*Expressions of Faith,* juried show, Old Stone Church, Cleveland, OH, Purchase Award
2003	*Drawings,* Massillon Museum, Massillon, OH
2007	*All Media Ohio,* Ashland College, Ashland, OH
2011	*Looking Inward,* invitational show, AAWR, Cleveland, OH
2012	*Celebration of Life,* Memorial Show, Walken Frame and Art Gallery, Cleveland, OH
2013	*Women VI,* Lakeland Community College, Kirtland, OH
2014	Solo Show, Intown Club, Cleveland, OH
	Women VII, Lakeland Community College, Kirtland, OH

Selected Collections

Archived member of the Artists Archives of the Western Reserve (AAWR), Cleveland, OH; Akron Children's Hospital, Akron, OH; Cleveland Zoological Society, Cleveland, OH; Jewish Community Center, Cleveland, OH; Jones, Day, Reavis & Pogue, Cleveland, OH; Kent State University, Kent, OH; Key Corporation National Bank, Cleveland, OH; MetroHealth Medical Center, Cleveland, OH; Myers and Company, Cleveland, OH; Plain Dealer Publishing Company, Cleveland, OH; Ronald McDonald House, Cleveland, OH; Stephen Paternity, Akron, OH

Publications

Spaces. *Drawings.* Exhibition catalog. Essay by Hilliard T. Goldfarb. Cleveland, OH, 1984.
The Cleveland Museum of Art. *The Bulletin of the Cleveland Museum of Art,* title page (66th May Show). Cleveland, OH, 1985.
Dialogue, An Art Journal. Cleveland, OH, May/June, 1981; March/April, 1984; January/February, 1986; May/June, 1986; November/December, 1986.
The Plain Dealer. Cleveland, OH, June 1985; January 9, 1986; September 14, 1986.
Plyler, Robert. "Images of Women Challenge, Intrigue, Delight," The Critical Eye. *The Post-Journal,* Saturday, July 12, 1986. Jamestown, NY
Waite, William. "Risks and Safeguards." *Chautauqua Art Association Galleries,* June 1986.
Cullinan, Helen. "16 Ohio artists in fine form." *The Plain Dealer,* November 5, 1986
Cullinan, Helen. "Capturing interaction between humans, apes." *The Plain Dealer,* July 1993.
Gray, Andy. "Shining a light on women in art." *Tribune Chronicle,* March 14, 1991.
University of Akron. *Drawing in Ohio at the Turn of the Century,* catalog. Akron, OH, 1995.
Litt, Steven. "Belief put on hold." *The Plain Dealer,* June 30, 1995.
University of Akron. *Drawings in Ohio at the Turn of the Century.* Exhibition catalog. Akron, OH, 1995.
In Good Company, a daily calendar. Cleveland: Pilgrim Press, 1996, 1997.
"Realism Today." *American Artist.* October 2000, p. 40 (illustration of "Winter" by Marilyn Szalay).
Cleveland Sight Center, Cleveland OH. "Dear in Winter Series," holiday cards to benefit Sight Center, 2013

JUDY TAKÁCS BIOGRAPHY
1962 -

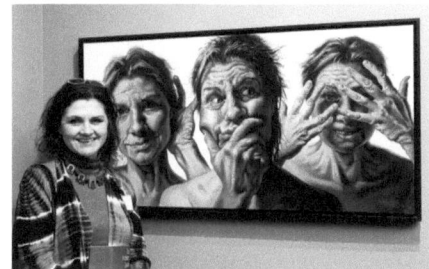

Biography

Takács received her BFA in Illustration and Portrait Painting from the Cleveland Institute of Art in 1986. Takács has staged serial projects painting senior citizens and elderly nuns from life. These projects have yielded over fifty paintings, three solo shows a feature in Anthropology & Aging Quarterly and placements in juried and invitational shows. In 2014 she published a book of these collected portraits of the elderly called, "The Age of Adventure."

In 2009 she began both painting and blogging her project; "Chicks with Balls: Judy Takács paints unsung female heroes." For this series, the artist asked her female friends and family to pose for her topless, holding balls to symbolize their personal challenges. In 2013, Takács authored and published, "Chicks with Balls: Judy Takács paints unsung female heroes." and received an Ohio Arts Council Grant for Individual Artistic Excellence for the series which is currently a traveling exhibition.

Takács' work has been recognized by the Portrait Society of America the Art Renewal Center, the National Arts Club, Cincinnati Arts Club, Allied Artists of America, Catharine Lorillard Wolf Club, and the Salmagundi Club, NYC. She has participated in Women Painting Women Exhibitions along with Rachel Constantine, Alia El-Bermani, Diane Fiesel and Sadie Valeri, and multiple Poets/Artists publications and live exhibitions. Takács' work is archived with historical Cleveland artists at the Artists Archives of the Western Reserve Her work has been exhibited at the Butler Institute of American Art the Zanesville Museum of Art, Evansville Museum, Museum of Contemporary Art Cleveland and ARTneo. Takács' work is included in the permanent collections of the Artists Archives of the Western Reserve, Susquehanna University and ARTneo.

In 2014, Takács curated "Majority Rising" for the Artists Archives of the Western Reserve during Women's History Month. Choosing work from Cleveland figurative artists, Shirley Aley Campbel, Kathleen McKenna, Marilyn Szalay, Lee Heinen and Marsha Sweet. Takács painted and exhibited a portrait of each artist as well.

In 2016 Takács was one of the nine artists, including Stephanie Deshpande, Lauren Tilden, Mario Robinson, and Terry Strickland, who participated in the Emanuel Nine Portrait Projec at Principle Gallery, honoring the victims of the Charleston Church Shooting. Takács is past chair of the New Media Relations sub-committee of the Portrait Society of America Cecilia Beaux Forum, and now holds a board position as Social Media Chair for the Allied Artists of America.

Takács' father is Queueing Theory pioneer, Lajos Takács, PhD and her mother, is Clear the Line and Refugee from Paradise, author, Dalma Takács, PhD.

Bibliography

Sight Unseen, February 2016, Didi Menendez, with curator Alia El-Bermani, Poets/Artists, Chicago, Illinois
The Archives Speak, November 2014, Rota Sackerlotzky and Roger Welchans, The Artists Archives of the Western Reserve, Cleveland, Ohio
Age of Adventure: Judy Takács paints the retired and inspired, August 2014, Judy Takács, blurb.com, Cleveland, Ohio
Women Painting Women, September 2014. Matter Deep Publishing, Principle Gallery, South Carolina
Art Renewal Center International Salon Catalog 2013/14. August 2014
Present Tense: Contemporary Art in Ohio, Artists of Rubber CIty. November 2014.
Manifest Gallery International Painting Annual 3. January 2014. Manifest Gallery, Cincinnati, Ohio
Chicks with Balls: Judy Takács paints unsung female heroes, August 2013, blurb.com
Solon Senior Project: Judy Takács paints fascinating wisdom, November 2012, blurb.com

www.ingramcontent.com/pod-product-compliance
Lightning Source LLC
Chambersburg PA
CBHW041935240526
45473CB00034B/1707